KO-HUA CHEN (1961–) is a prolific and multi-award-winning Taiwanese writer. He has published over thirty works of poetry, prose, drama, and film criticism. Chen was Taiwan's first openly gay poet: his work has contributed to a remarkable flourishing of LGBT literature within this country. He lives in Taipei, where he works as an ophthalmologist.

WEN-CHI LI is an authority on queer literature in Taiwan; aside from his translations of LGBT poets, he also edited the first-ever anthology of queer poetry in Taiwan. He is the co-editor of the volume *Taiwanese Literature as World Literature* (Bloomsbury, 2022) and the cofounder of the 'World Literature from Taiwan' series at Balestier Press. He is currently Susan Manning Fellow at the University of Edinburgh, after acquiring a PhD in sinology from the University of Zurich in 2022.

COLIN BRAMWELL is a poet and translator from the north of Scotland. He was the runner-up in the 2020 Edwin Morgan Poetry Award, and is currently working towards a doctorate in creative writing at the University of St Andrews. He and Wen-chi Li won the 2018 John Dryden Translation Competition for their translations of the Taiwanese poet Yang Mu.

THE PRIDE LIST

EDITED BY SANDIP ROY AND BISHAN SAMADDAR

The Pride List presents works of queer literature to the world. An eclectic collection of books of queer stories, poems, plays, biographies, histories, thoughts, ideas, experiences and explorations, the Pride List does not focus on any specific region, nor on any specific genre, but celebrates the great diversity of LGBTQ+ lives across countries, languages, centuries and identities, with the conviction that queer pride comes from its unabashed expression.

ALSO IN **THE PRIDE LIST**

KIM HYUN
Glory Hole
Translated from the Korean by
Suhyun J. Ahn and Archana Madhavan

MICHAŁ WITKOWSKI
Eleven-Inch
Translated from the Polish by W. Martin

DANISH SHEIKH
Love and Reparation
A Theatrical Response to the Section 377 Litigation in India

CYRIL WONG
Infinity Diary

MU CAO
In the Face of Death We Are Equal
Translated from the Chinese by
Scott E. Myers

PAWAN DHALL
Out of Line and Offline
Queer Mobilizations in '90s Eastern India

MIREILLE BEST
Camille in October
Translated from the French by
Stephanie Schechner

Ko-hua Chen

DECAPITATED POETRY

TRANSLATED BY

Wen-chi Li and **Colin Bramwell**

LONDON CALCUTTA NEW YORK

Sponsored by the Ministry of Culture, Taiwan

Seagull Books, 2023

First published in Chinese in 1995

First published in English translation by Seagull Books, 2023

ISBN 978 1 80309 1 648

British Library Cataloguing-in-Publication Data
A catalogue record for this book is available from the British Library

Cover designed by Sunandini Banerjee, Seagull Books, Calcutta, India, using two photographs by Dev Asangbam, obtained under licence from unsplash.com

Book designed by Bishan Samaddar, Seagull Books, Calcutta, India
Photographs reproduced on pages 1 and 65 are by Ekaterina Kuznetsova and Inge Poelman respectively, obtained under licence from unsplash.com

Printed and bound in the USA by Versa Press

Contents

TWO SCI-FI SEQUENCES

INTRODUCTION

Ko-hua Chen's *Decapitated Poetry* was first published in Chinese in 1995: a period in Taiwanese history which saw the remarkable blossoming of LGBTQ art in that country. Chen's work can certainly be seen as part of the movement, including works such as Chu Tien-wen's *Notes of a Desolate Man* (1994), Chi Ta-wei's *The Membranes* (1995) and Qiu Miaojin's twin masterpieces *Notes of a Crocodile* (1994) and *Last Words from Montmartre* (1996), and films like Ang Lee's *The Wedding Banquet* (1993). As ever, the efforts of queer and pro-queer writers and artists reflected a degree of grassroots social activism. This decade also saw the establishment of the country's first halfway house for HIV patients, as well as the first gay and lesbian societies, gay radio programmes, queer publishing houses, and even one LGBTQ Presbyterian Church. At present, Taiwan is the only country in Asia to have fully legalized same-sex marriage—an astonishing landmark for gay rights in the region that certainly could not have taken place without the breathtaking milieu of queer culture that emerged in this nation in the 1990s.

It is hard to underestimate the significance of this moment for Taiwanese literature and culture—and for queer culture in Asia in general. Eight years before the publication of *Decapitated Poetry*, Taiwan had fully embraced democracy for the first time in its history. From 1947 to 1987, Taiwanese citizens had lived under the American-backed dictatorship begun by Chiang Kai-shek and upheld through his Chinese Nationalist Party, the Kuomintang (KMT). Inaugurated by the massacres of the February 28th Incident in 1947, Taiwanese citizens lived under a state of martial law for forty years. During what would be later termed the 'White Terror', free speech was prohibited, public assemblies banned, elections controlled, and outspoken intellectuals imprisoned or murdered. Homosexuality was—and, to a large extent, still is—taboo in East Asian society, but Taiwan's diplomatic proximity to the USA led to the widespread importing of Western medical terminologies for sexuality. The American Psychiatric Association's designation of homosexuality as a 'sociopathic personality disturbance' in the 1950s became influential in Taiwanese medical circles. As the century progressed, Taiwan (like many other countries around the world) also fell under the influence of resurgent American fundamentalist Christianity. Justifiably fearing reprisal, queer writers stayed in the closet. Ko-Hua Chen would be the first Taiwanese poet to leave it.

Ko-Hua Chen was born in 1961, in Hualien, a seaside city that is famous for being the birthplace of several important Taiwanese poets, notably Chen Li (1954–) and Yang Mu (1940–2020). Since graduating from university, he has balanced a highly productive literary career with his work as an ophthalmologist. Remarkably, Chen's sci-fi masterpiece 'Notes on a Planet' was written while the poet was still a teenager. The poem contains a fascinating interplay between queer identity and technology and tells the story of an unrequited love between a homosexual narrator and his straight friend. The disruptions of bodily unity that post-human technology creates—cloning, genetic modification, robotics, interstellar travel—allowed Chen to describe a world where human subjectivity and societal unity both undergo comparable processes of fragmentation. Organic existence in a mechanical world poses similar ontological questions to contemporaneous queer existence in heteronormative societies. When these societies appear in 'Notes', they tend to be dystopian, objects of satire. For instance, in the section 'A Mixed-Race Baby', the narrator recalls being manufactured and assigned with the mission of 'bat[ting] for the other side': a process involving 'worshipping the national philosophy that gave birth to Nazism and Beethoven's right ear', 'analysing the operational definition of love' and ultimately 'pioneering virginity reconstruction surgery'. However, the majority of the poem takes place on a different planet, where narrator and lover exist together in splendid isolation. 'Notes on a Planet' received the China Times Award for Narrative Poetry in 1981, but was not published until 1987, two months after martial law was lifted. Readers today will still find the poem to be a relevant examination of issues surrounding technology, love and identity: it has aged well and could easily have been written in the present day. The satire is so outlandish and multidirectional that the reader's attention is directed to the world Chen creates, rather than to its queer subtext. However, this subtext is certainly present.

Decapitated Poetry, published eight years later, was a far riskier affair: in these poems, Chen spoke with unparalleled directness about the realities of contemporaneous homosexual life in Taiwan. Moreover, *Decapitated Poetry* took aim at a heteronormative society which is simultaneously fascinated with and disgusted by queer eroticism; establishing a satirical mode begun by 'Notes on a Planet', but switching genres, from sci-fi to a form of realism. The most famous poem in the collection, 'The Necessity of Anal Sex', addresses heterosexual male readers directly, encouraging them to explore sex with other men. The description of homosexual identity in this poem—and generally throughout the book—deliberately flirts with voyeurism, in a way that is designed to not only shock straight readers but also to widen their sense of the divergent forms that sex can take. Gay men are described as 'twitching like rats [. . .] under a light-focussing magnifier', 'our body hair so blood-soaked it looks like / someone has spilled a bottle of red hair dye over us'. The tenor of these descriptions, and of Chen's poetry in this vein more generally, may remind readers of the Marquis de Sade, an important figure for Chen. No Taiwanese writer had written so explicitly about homosexual sex before—or since. The book was controversial. However, *Decapitated Poetry* was intended as much for contemporaneous queer readers (whether closeted or not) as for straight ones. Chen certainly represents many facets of queerness explicitly, but this explicitness also has a demystifying effect. Below the veneer of difference, the romantic encounters depicted by Chen here involve as much affection, lust and melancholy as any other. This observation is as true for the sci-fi poems as it is for Chen's more corporeal work.

*

As translators, we felt that it was important to give a sense of the broadness of Chen's output as a writer. A contrast between the earthly and the astral in Chen seemed, to us, to be a good way of communicating this. Chen is an astonishingly productive writer: he has published over thirty books in his lifetime and received many awards for his poetry as well as for his song lyrics. This book selects work from across Chen's career, which is presented thematically, rather than in order of publication. We begin with selections from *Decapitated Poetry*; the works after 'Body Poems' are selected from later collections, and include 'The Necessity of Bestiality', a laugh-out-loud demolition of the now-cliché fundamentalist Christian argument that gay marriage will lead to bestiality. Chen's speculative epic 'Notes on a Planet' appears at the end of the book and is preceded by the 2009 poem 'Twelve Love Songs for a Cyborg'. This sequence neatly bridges some of the satirical-sociological concerns of the corporeal poems from *Decapitated Poetry* (and later in Chen's career) as well as the 'hard' sci-fi world of 'Notes'. We think that this selection illustrates Chen's poetry at its best—controversial, illuminating, formally daring, and far ahead of its time—perhaps even ahead of ours.

Wen-chi Li and Colin Bramwell

DECAPITATED POETRY

Song of Dumbbells

I come back to the dumbbells.
I think I can hear them chanting.
I even start to chant along with them.
The room is completely silent, of course.

The silence of these dumbbells echoes
the bottomless dark of our planet,
its alluring, tacit cry. My silence is of
gums and gnashing teeth—

firmly, unrevealing of
spiritual weakness, I breathe
                                        I sigh.

I do not show my pride.
I never say anything.
I face the dumbbells

as though they were my fate.
I turn back to them, to first positions.
My eyelashes droop with humility—
or defiant majesty, perhaps.
Using them feels like picking up a medal,
then dropping it again, over and over.

The earth is round
but the ground is flat.
No contradiction there.
Soft muscles,
hard bones in-between.
I turn away from the mirror,
set the dumbbells down.
They intone their soft song
silent and heavy and deaf
to the one my teeth sing back.

Like a tree returning to the soil,
like a cloud returning to a window,
like glory emanating from a crown,
like a slogan held in closing knuckles,
like a dream meandering back towards wet lashes,
like memory to a callow shoulder,
I will always come back to these dumbbells
that today are chanting so gently their song
that cannot be heard by the world.

From the Treadmill, I Can See . . .

From my treadmill, I can see a carousel slowing down.
A black horse loses pace and dies.
A gaudy horse loses pace and dies.
A horse the colour of wine loses pace and dies.
A water horse loses pace and dies.
A foggy horse loses pace and dies.
A grass horse loses pace and dies . . .

On this treadmill, I walk my tortured trail.
Life is a pasture piled high with dead horses.
I am the only one capable
of counting my own heartbeats
when passing through the endless
charnel house of these plains.
This was revealed to me in my last dream.
In the pasture of life, among the fallen steeds,
I am the last one standing.

I am the final horse on this carousel,
refusing to concede that the scene
    will repeat,
even in the twinkling of an eye
        —will repeat and repeat.

House of the Mirror

Nothing's in this house but mirrors.

A man walks in
and sees himself whole:
the whole front side of him
that has been missing since childhood.

He will never be aware that
it is not his real self in the mirror, but his host.
He should have said hello to this figure,
taken off his hat, commenced with small talk.

Instead he blusters in,
drops his keys,
kicks off his shoes,
smiles,
then flexes his muscles.

The mirror responds:
all of my answers are written on your body.
Only the body fails to understand this.
The room is spacious and clean,
like nothing in the mind.
The mirror's silence is so bright,
a momentary shield from emptiness.

Fat. Fat is our common enemy.
This slogan provokes a small
army of narcissists into being.
They wave their flags loudly,
see their swollen selves reflected,
an immediate turn-on.

The house of the mirror is the soul's
final resting place . . .

Here his body quietly makes camp
and prays tomorrow's crossing will be safe.

No one discusses death, or the afterlife,
but they don't talk about life, either.
They are ashamed to love it.

Ode to Muscles

Biceps. Do you love me?
Soleus muscle. Hoorah, hoorah, hooray!
Quadriceps. People are the true masters of the nation.
Pectoralis major. Home, sweet home.
Vaginal contractions. Throw it away.
Orbicularis oculi. Our motherland is so magnificent.
Gastrocnemius. Are you happy? It's wonderful.
Superior oblique muscle. Superlative sex position.
Anal sphincter. Disposable tableware, Tylenol, hair restorative.
Abdominal muscle. Patriotism: love of the people, the party.
Latissimus dorsi muscle. Let me tell you about our national hero.
Corrugator supercilii muscle. A smile is the lubricant of interpersonal
relationships.
Arrector pili muscle. One, two, three, Taiwan!
Arm muscle. Popularity keeps you in good shape.
Upper frontalis muscle. Follow in the footsteps of God.
Levator muscle. Victory first: an excellent situation.
Extensor carpi radialis muscle. Obey, obey, or obey.
Masticatory muscles. Pillow, nipple, fist.
Kissing muscles. Do you ever feel empty?
Triceps. Sweet fuck all.

An Invisible Murder

Last night a dumbbell went missing from the gym.
We cannot yet confirm it has been murdered—
the autopsy shows a small tilt in the spine,
some deformed cartilage, compressed nerves,
disagreement in the yoke muscles—

but no one as yet has come forward
to identify the dumbbell's corpse.
We believe it may be hidden within the skull of a silent man.
There are signs that rape may have occurred,
but none of the usual evidence:
semen, nails, fingerprints
have not been found.

We're currently following leads on a mirror
who must have witnessed the whole process—
the victim has an identical twin,
but the question of who is lonelier cannot be confirmed—
and all mirrors are as clear as new mirrors,
their faces innocent,
virginal.

The Death of the Last Bodybuilder

He raises the dumbbell, as though to strike, then throws it down.
It was his weapon. When those old warriors
who wield knives, sticks, nunchucks and the rest
pile up at his feet,
he cannot help but think
that he must be invincible.
It's certainly a unique fighter
who uses such modest, hard armaments.

Under the sway of his mighty brawn
other weapons and bodies bend like reeds in the wind.
Victory and defeat, dominance and submission, are such disparate ends.
In his heart he questions the point of living this way:
surrounded by such wretched company, surely all his triumphs are stale.
People are ordinary, goofy and full of schemes,
and all of them will fall before his dumbbell,
which he raises again now, imagining that he is in a desolate place
a place that even the ants flee from—
a misty wood.
He walks into this wood
and sees a giant tree, its thousand-year-old trunk
standing like a dark-faced *arhat*, ascetic with shut eyes.
He roars and throws his weapons into the air—

The earth stumbles.
Gravity was his nemesis all along.

He takes a few steps forward, thuds.
White brains splash in the godly wood.
Two dumbbells—heavy, gory, pointless—
stick out from his skull.

This Morning after We Fuck

This morning after we fuck
I'll leave on a jet plane.
This morning after we fuck
I'll depart on a rocket ship.
This morning after we fuck
I'll say goodbye and hitch a ride on a UFO.
This morning after we fuck,
I'll ride your unconscious out of here.
(You'll not be woken.)
This morning after we fuck

the earth leaves. Weights stay.
Desire leaves. Weights stay.
The morning leaves. Weights stay.
Tomorrow leaves. Weights stay.
I leave.

I Am Curious about My Body

I complete my nudity,
become accustomed to it.
As my lips are lucid
they cannot help but kiss me back
(nor can I help but kiss me back).
Under the terms of my contract, I must
mate with the camera for at least thirty minutes.
A fig leaf that God has forgotten about
doesn't quite cover my cock.

I kiss myself in a shop window
as though it were a stunt;
hitherto I had never practised
how to erect a big toe.

But I can point out an inconvenient truth.
A thousand different varieties of bodily fluids seep into my blood,
overwhelming my sensitive, accurate interior.
My truth is so obscene, brutal and deadly
like bodily fluids intermingling,
exuding their overripe sweetness . . .

Let saliva dissolve acid steel and rust!
Let cum dry in the cracked bed of the lips!
Let sputum mix with pollen and fish eggs

and rush into the vast ocean!
Let tears devour the eyeballs!
Blindness? Bring it on!

Vow

My dearest love,
thankyou for buying me this expensive ring:
from hereon out, I authorize you
to use my cunt.

In turn, you will feed me with
mapo tofu, burgers and fries, sushi,
kimchi, dim sum, *dejeuner*—
and, of course, with your cock and your spunk
your toes, your body hair
your STIs, your genital warts, my darling . . .

Did I mention that I have an honours degree?
I am mature and financially independent.
From this day on, I will be your only wife:
and if anyone should accuse me of ever having touched
other similarly swollen veiny penises before, I shall deny it.
I will forget everything about my father:
only admire the shape of *your* throat,
the reek of *your* pits, from now on.

I promise to never ever ever stop dieting. Or exercising,
though I draw the line at giving up on soaps,
and will never cease masturbating,
not even if you ask me nicely.

I used to cherish my hymen:
these days my vaginal sphincter's quite well worked out.
I think all of us are guilty of misunderstanding
what 'virginity' really means . . .
My dearest love: in return for this, our contract,
please accept my leather whip, my branding iron,
my handcuffs, my cock-and-ball torture equipment,
and three jars of water-based lubricant.

Oh, how much I love you, dear,
but if you were an SS officer in black, I'd love you more.
Never mind! After our snow-white wedding's done, my love,
I will pray to God for a hairy little baby who looks just like you
who will bite my milky tits, and squeeze them till they burst.
Oh, I just can't wait! I'm the happiest girl in the world! I do!

The Necessity of Anal Sex

we wake from our resplendent
opening night
to find that a back door has been left unlocked,

to find that wombs and bowels are essentially the same room,
separated only by a tepid wall:

we dance among the aphrodisiac flowers in bloom
our limbs unfolding tenderly, our skins
in contact, two brand-new species touching:
before the mortal storm of history,
not even Freud could have predicted our bliss:

we are a brand-new species
exempt from poverty athletic injury and AIDS

let us expose our asses and our consciences alike:
naked under a light-focussing magnifier
ready for inspection:
observe us twitching like rats
empathize with our painful joy
our body hair so blood-soaked it looks like someone
has spilled a bottle of red hair dye over us:

oh, will we ever have the luck
to prove the necessity of anal sex
within in our short lifespans?
we must get home before the back door locks:

this bed will lead us to the grave:
another glorious day of betrayal:
no one knows what putrefying reason
is concealed in a sutured wound:
why don't we just bleed out?

he who said he wanted to corrupt
all morality is the first to leave the group:
he dances in a dense sea of flowers,
brandishing his halo,
and even he is unable to prove
that anal sex isn't necessary:

as the back door will always remain unlocked
sorrow often leaks through it
like a light bulb flickering on and off all night:
we hold and hold each other
and refuse to believe that all our methods of making love have
been exhausted
the joys of the flesh abandoned:
why don't we join the silent, healthy majority?
why can't we devote our lives to the majority?

majority: good
sleep: good
sex: good
no sex: also good

whatever: know this, heterosexual male reader:
whether you knock politely
or force your way into our house
these parts of us will always remain
forever open:

Man Eats Man

When dinner lands on the table, you ask:
What's this we're having, then?
A soup made from your heart and your liver, I reply.

It's hard to keep human flesh ripe,
though my main problem is that I'm a lousy cook and you know it.
Often my brains are too bland, my loin a bit fishy,
the eyeballs far too firm,
dirty fingernails floating on the surface.

Human flesh is said to be delicious.
You look in your hollowed-out chest,
caress your insatiable belly, complain.
No fingerbones to pick your teeth.

Invisible Man

You can't see me, just as you can't see the truth
that walks beside you. But you think about me often.
Audit me. Write about me.
Try to identify me. Master me. Use me, whatever.
But you are approaching a two-dimensional problem
with a three-dimensional attitude.
I am a creature whose only concept is of flatness.
I can only walk between the straight lines of words on the page,
I take my shelter in the sophisticated lobes of a more advanced species.
I am neither holy grail of power nor world-changing wand.
I'm more like a nervous rabbit: fragile, alert, edible, always ready to bolt.
I am an invisible man hiding in the second dimension.
Don't search for my whereabouts on a computer terminal.
Don't look for my image in the public library.
When the castle you build in the sky finally collapses
under the unbearable weight of its staggering lies,
perhaps among the rubble of shattered ideologies
you will catch a glimpse of my swift fleeting body,
dashing through the end-of-century wastelands.

Fly Man

I just don't understand why those cigar-biting, becalculatored, golden-
bow-tied Hollywood bigshots chose me,
chose to mix my genes with those of a human.
My tiny, black chromosomes are filled with cryptic, bloodthirsty,
greedy, carnivorous data.
My saliva's as mellow as lager-foam, my body hair stiff as metal springs:
I am nothing like a human.
Humans also lack a pair of compound eyes that can overrule the brain,
and they aren't nearly as good at attracting attention,
and my sexual appetite's significantly more voracious—but most
importantly of all,
I am pretty good at spreading implicit but unspoken truths with my
flapping wings. Listen:

buzz buzz buzz
buzz
buzz buzz
buzz buzz
buzz
buzz buzz
buzz
buzz buzz

(All molecular
biologists
listen attentively
but fail to comprehend
the ultimate meaning of
the human-fly hybrid
and its relationship
to capitalism)

Yeah.
I don't know. Maybe Hollywood was right.
Maybe humans haven't produced enough garbage yet.
Buzz, buzz, buzz, buzz . . .

Toilet Man

He is happy to have a choice of commodes in the morning.
After inspecting all the toilet bowls closely, he chooses his favourite
and sits.
He's sure that nature will be calling soon.
He recalls eating nothing yesterday, except a vitamin B pill, a small
carton of barley tea,
half a pint of noxious antiseptic mouthwash, a little squeeze of
Colgate, and his own saliva.
Then he shits profusely, as well he might.
Man is truly a stinking, excremental creature.
As it all came out, the thought crossed his mind.
He really hadn't eaten anything at all.
His soul quietly stands up, ascends from his body.
It rises into the toilet above, and finds the showers.
Is heaven next door? it asks, as the water comes on.
The soul knocks on the wall to its left.
The water answers back. It makes a flushing noise.
Soon he is dizzy from swirling around,
and it sounds like someone's about to burst into song.

Snake Man

All I did was carry out God's will. For this, I was punished.

He wanted to teach himself how to walk on his belly. Initially, he designed a simple geometrical pattern to follow: then, despite all of the many obstacles in his way, he learned this pattern by heart. Soon enough the glowing sapphire of his form was snaking a sticky trail across the chequered tiles, like a scarf left by the god of night. Not another soul has set foot in this deserted Eden since. Punishment became a game; the snake's body simplified over time.

But now we too are wriggling forward, backbones following front-bones, as though on an invisible track, anticipating an encounter with light and music in the far distance. Belly-walking is central to our way of being. It brings our aesthetic practice full circle. Our dazzling venom leaps into the void: our hero gracefully curls towards his death, having embraced a form of idiocy quite unlike any other.

Ten Condom Commandments

1: Sex = Condoms

Even in that bygone age, his desire
        was still negligible,
his sense of self was intact,
pleasure felt pure. He still believed

in the unity of soul and body.

He prayed too
always reciting, loudly:
and Solomon slept
with his fathers.

2: Use It from the Exact Moment Intercourse Starts

Some of us treat the idea of falling in love with pure disdain.
They just keep making love
                throwing it away
                making love
                throwing it away
                making love.

Good Samaritans
always repenting,
trying to make a better life—

3: Choose Your Brand Carefully

Doing so without getting an erection is almost impossible.

4: Negotiate the Various Flavours and Sizes

He finally admits that sex
as he understands it
is ugly
corporeal
supplementary
discontinuous
beyond face value
full of punctuation
variation
xx
epoché

5: Don't Be Afraid to Put a New One On

The unity of soul and body.
Of course the soul has nothing to do with body, as in:

chicken and rabbit
fire and water
penis and cunt

6: Always Carry One with You

Orgasm. Orgasm. Orgasm
(futile repetition)
like emotions
being over-nourished
curdling too easily.

7: Discard after Use

Don't get bored of putting one on.
Can't get bored of putting one on.
Won't get bored of putting one on.
Not bored.
            He stands
in front of the mirror
looking at himself
feeling inspiration as flame
as desire
building momentum.

8: Do Not Use with Oil-Based Lubricant

Latex?
Anaesthetic cream?
Redemption?
Spermicidal?
Long live AIDS.

9: Featherlight for Greater Sensitivity

He caresses his plastic skin
desiring the long-lost liberation of sweat.
His fingertips feel the touch of dreams,
finally he understands—and it has taken him long enough—

the condom has become part of the body.

10: Always Use Condoms

Always use condoms.

Rain

I am a burning drop of rain falling from a blistered cloud:
I aim to land on your exposed chest, your nipples.
Wake now from your shameful sleep!
Wake into perverted passions,
cruel palms, horny hair;
wake into your dissimulating conscience
your empty memories and 'esoteric' tattoos.
Your opponents are demonstrating outside,
moving the world closer to chaotic dreams of yours.
Politicians and tycoons are just like us:
their disgraceful slogans penetrate your consciousness
like a whole battalion of insects.
And still you do not wake.
(When it starts to bucket down, I will dismiss my troops.)
Why aren't you afraid of me?
Your shameless, dreaming forehead
has ignored the revelation of my single
dropping life, but I am the embodiment
of trillions of raindrops sent by God
to flood the Earth in Noah's time.
I fear the chaos of my own destruction.
But you, my darling—my lover and nothing else besides—
what do you fear?

Map of a Wet Dream

when the little prince meets another little prince
when the black knight duels with the white knight
when a faucet looks down a plughole
when a thumb caresses a little finger

when gold melts lead
when sweat passes through tears
when his lips leap into her labia
when an abstract picture hangs inside an abstract picture

when trembling piles up with trembling
when waves are decorated with waves
when a scream pierces another scream
when the present reflects the present

but not its essence

when breath tries to grip breath
when forces are in tension
when shadows evade shadows
when poison dilutes another cup of poison

when a planet orbits a planet
when nothingness is emptied of nothingness

when a door opens a door
when the time dreams of itself

when death duplicates death
when one pleasure extinguishes another
when one pleasure simulates another
when the penis tip beats on the nipple

he is dreaming
that he is king dreaming
of a place that was his life
below white
mortal sheets

A Son of Emptiness

The youngest son of a prisoner on death row
is wandering, a ghost,
a beast emerging from its cave.
With a disproportionate sense of melancholy for someone his age
he looks sideways at the pallid world,
his thin shoulders overloaded by the shadow of his fate

pushing him into his own bone-white corner.
Once his father held a whip, a broken bottle high,
but now the boy fears nothing.
His tears wander far from their home.
Death is tucked into the pocket of his shorts,
silently growing hard between unscrubbed nails and skin.

Though love and hate often pass him by,
most of the time he feels numb.
The giant vines of nightmares and love
imprisoned in the grave
will grow into the labyrinth of his bones . . .

Yes, at moments he is elevated by his indifference.
At moments he is strong and brave.
But never is he not the youngest son of a prisoner on death row.
His memory is as strong as his birthmark.
No one learns to tolerate him.
He learns to focus more on himself:

gets some voyeuristic ink done,
admires Momotarō, who was fed at a monster's breast.

Does he still remember the taste of his mother's milk?
In folklore, he enjoys ascending the brown, oily mountain
but forgets how to latch onto the nipple at the top.
His sad lips can no longer sing the song of greeting gods.
Why don't you satisfy me with your wound, little death . . . ?
And sometimes he is weak grass waiting to be watered with blood:

toothy grass, a poisoned wall,
earrings with hidden daggers, an oath ring,
a bruised scrotum, diamond-cut pupils,
dancing servants,
nonexistent hearts.
Why not braid your hair
like a warrior before battle?

Crusted palms.
Feet that kiss the stone.
Universally hurtful rhetoric.
Gorgeous garments.
Strong eloquent tongue.
Mean coercive teeth.
Dying eyebrows.

Son of emptiness,
nihilist son, why do you bother
to wipe away your tears?

Why do you still refuse
to name your father?

Body Poems (*Selected*)

Tongue

A radical body-materialist
sticks out his tongue
articulating a lotus
that glares from the very tip.

Tell me something sweet, you say.
Love needs sweetness,
politics needs sweetness,
power needs sweetness.
Family, friendships, one-night stands
relationships
all need a bit of sweetness—

I must wake
the tender, savoury animal
lying flat in your mouth
half-cooked by a salivary steam.

After our kiss
all of me cannot stop
thinking about it.

In reality it's just another tongue.

Chest

What I aspire to is
a wideness of thick soil
and the graceful and soothing breath of the planet beneath it—

the macho upsurge
from abdomen
to neck
mountains above, oceans beneath—

my secret heart sails
to the middle of a quiet sea.
When the moon is fully eclipsed
and the stars are blind in the dark
I lie flat on the upper deck,
and the sea's surface looks like it's been lacquered,
and I am giddy.

Clinging to the earth's chest,
I become aware of a vehement pulse that echoes through the universe.

I love you so much,
I circulate my blood
with your breath.

When the moonlight shines on my bare chest again
all stars dim and deviate from their orbits.

Nipple

Why do men have nipples?
This is the headline of today's newspaper—

on my table, two poached eggs,
creamy yolks on a white plate
waiting to be licked clean.

Under a white shirt
protruding
(evolution of man)
like two unexploded mines
left on a battlefield—

fingers tap and pinch
two rodent incisors
clamp down—

look—
how imperfect they are,

these soft
erected spheres.

Spine

Deep in the vast territory of your back
an ancient, elongated fossil,
a centipede-like arthropod sinks,

crouching quietly under your skin.
Sometimes it can be seen
showing off the primeval
verve of its vigour,
like an extraterrestrial parasite.

All internal organs are suspended from the spine.
Yes, the spine bears the heaviness of
all your organs and faculties and senses
and—yes—marks the evolution of our species
from crawling to standing on two legs.

Finally, you are standing up.
Finally, we stand up, kiss,
we fuck face-to-face.

The ancient, elongated arthropod
that lives within your body—
I dive for it.

Foreskin

Nerves reach past the bladder
further
descending
a few inches away—

suddenly interrupted.
Are you not circumcised?
The expression in his eyes confuses me.
When I stand under
the showerhead's raining net
performing ablutions within the ostentatious
flower of my crotch,
a tight, physical comfort is felt there.

I question whether I ought
to exchange this organ for the blue-blooded
name on an ID badge.
                                        Now my finger circles
          the scar
around his smooth and passionate kernel—
its mysterious, cosmic apogee—
the core of all meaning.

Belly Button

The sea undulates, breathing
I sail I sink into
a deep whirlpool

like the Beagle spacecraft
drifting towards an island of black holes
at the centre of it all

warm fragile ticklish
cold intolerant

I kiss this whirlpool
and am sucked into its singularity

I crumble into light

a tsunami trembles in the distance—
no, it is the universe that sneezes.

Glans

Mine is mellow, plump,
bright red, a little purple, juicy—
he reads this description on the online dating profile.
It sticks out from the others.
His attention is diverted to it—

he thought this man meant nipples or lips
—in fact you could describe any sexual organ this way:
the nose, the toes, etc.

But among all human parts, he says,
quietly, gracefully,
I still prefer—
the tip.

Genitals

A country where all humans are equal,
and genitals are treated like the organs of the face:
reflecting personality, mood, age, secrets.

A country where all are allowed to love,
to hide their privates in their hands,
to rub away at the beautifully hirsute
and private minefield that for all becomes as moist
as the miasma of a deeply buried,
decomposing mole.

And as we are a species that loves philosophy,
loves to sacrifice ourselves for the greater good—
a species that meditates on how to improve the world,
so that collectively we all might reach
a state of peace, fairness and equality—

all genitals must eventually be made
public, formulaic, common.
The law will forbid one person
from having two cunts or two cocks,
or one cunt and one cock.
Only one cunt or one cock will be allowed.
This law will be rigorously policed
and all deviants thoroughly whipped.

Genitals should represent the generosity of love.

Love is wordless.
It always returns to its unsolvable contradictions.

Love is selfless,
all private markings indicate an unresolvable betrayal.

Love should be selfless.
I say genitals are great and free and empty.

Long live the genitals, long live the genitals, long live.

Prostate

Beneath the auspices of an exam,
my fingers enter his anus
and touch his prostate.

Soft and shy,
vulnerable,
absolutely male.
A mysterious gland
hidden in a part of the body
that is unspeakable—

only through the anus
can a finger
reach it.

God has buried this gland
in secret
like a middle-aged man
having trouble taking a leak:

hidden in the small of his bowels
a feeling of being pressed
of being right at the edge of it.

Thigh

Back then, the men
would go to heaven to bathe.
I was a child.

Their thighs were a forest
I travelled through,
pagoda bedposts
so large and thick that
I could barely hold on to them.
Then I practised climbing,
hanging from the horizontal bar.

I felt the warm mist from the mountains
like a hot spring erupting over me.
The smell was that of ancient, masculine sweat,
a pheromone that urged me
grow up soon, kid—

In the end, I completely lost myself
in the forest of thighs.

I am still lost there. Even today
I am compelled once again
to search the canopy
for loaded, swollen fruit.

Calf

It's like a flounder
hidden under the skin of a calf

sliding   shrinking
maintaining still
repeating again—
how tasty this fish looks.

It flirts with me, a shark
in the hot   brined air.

I shuttle to it,
ravenous.

I Love the Founding Father

Like a whore with a crush on her local policeman
I love our Founding Father so much. Day and night
I allow his citizens in and out of my body.
And when I'm spent I offer up my wages
to a young and chiselled officer of the law.

He has a short beard. He speaks loudly, often with his hands.
He writes official documents using simple language.
He has two eyelids, he is of medium stature
his upper lip is thin but strong
and passionate and ideal and seems not to fear death.

After I hand him my money he always gives me
the customary lecture, encouraging me to both
dedicate myself to and be delighted by my whoring,
to always stick with what I know.
Do something great, my dear.
Once he told me:
Your ○ is big, my ● is big too.
I imagine the fact that we are fucking
is quite a big deal for you.

I used to feel a sort of despair in my love
for him. Whenever I was in the school
gymnasium, after assembly, I felt it.

Now every time I see his shadow
I recall my choice of profession.

My breasts have been promoted to his inner circle.
His knowledge is like a massive foreign frigate.
I love our Founding Father . . .

And my customers, exhausted,
lying on top of me love what I have whispered to them.
In my most philosophical but encouraging tone of voice,
I always say the following phrase:

The revolution has not yet succeeded, comrades.
You must remain vigilant. Your labour must continue.

Works every time.

Bareback, Cool?

A flower dons a cap in the middle of the night
to avoid polluting the world with its fragrance at daybreak.

When mountains wear white caps to resist the cold
you walk to my nakedness,
trying to transform your own into another kind.

As a pillow puts on a pillowcase before bed
we remove our eye masks, earplugs, hair nets.
Our nipples are like two glossy metallic switches:
once pressed, the world blacks out.
You remove the curtains, wallpapers, carpets
and cut them into the shape of a man's body
to prevent our cacti from growing excessively large.
You say, *this is just to prevent bleeding in penetration.*
But my middle finger, erected by all the cursing,
has already been caught in a trap of untruths,
and sings like a racist to a gory swamp.

fuck, fuck, fuck fuck and fuck
my country my home
fuck everyone

I decide to suspend my nakedness.
If I am to sheathe myself somehow,

can I just leave all my clothes on and poke
my penis out of my trousers,
or must I slip into the far more
depressing semi-nudity of a prophylactic?

I decide not to decide
just let the elephant's trunk define my physicality,
the natural smell of bananas
overwhelm my interlocutor's olfactory instincts.

I say: pleasure is necessary,
but slogans make me impotent.
Condoms are like government informers,
like Nazi salutes,
like fascist pamphlets,
like campaign ads on television.
They are everywhere and they want
to castrate the erogenous zones of my body.

I say a stream chooses to flow to a lower place:
not to be the lower place.

Not all the birds on the higher
branches become dominant.

It's still possible to be careless
while wearing a condom.

But I want you to wear one.

Oh well, if you insist . . .

Your Scrotum Tightens Up

Your scrotum tightens and tightens again
showing the wrinkles of an ageing terrain
a fine mineral structure, crystalline—my tongue
traces all the way to the root of this giant mushroom
like a boy from a fairy tale by the Brothers Grimm
who bravely runs away from home
and dares to grow lascivious in adulthood.

Images, endless images
such a visually oriented man . . .
I cannot get away from
the desire to swallow or be penetrated.
After rain, faint sun.
I chant a spell: grow, mushroom, harder!

I'm coming. I'm coming . . .
The truth of life will be revealed
in one enormous spreading ooze
like a piston pounding between
my throat and soft palate
blocking my voice.

Then fountains,
fountains everywhere
everyone, anywhere, to save everything—

to cleanse it all again, the first purge will be
of the groin of the soul but someone

has already started to pull up his trousers.
His flesh still exhausted in the depths of trench-warfare sheets
he is already pulling up his designer underwear
that tightly wraps his slowly descending sack
that's sculpted with neat mysterious
divinations, totems reflecting
the ancient, fading memories of mankind . . .

Every tragedy
begins with a pair of testicles
contracting
slowly

sadly
drooping

end-
less
slow-
ly
droo-
ping

I Want You to Swim in My Body

I want you to swim in my body.
I want you to learn to swim in my body.
But first you must fall in love with the water . . .
Come, dive into my body
bravely dive into the depth of my body
make waves fill your ears
eyes mouth and nostrils with me
take a deep breath hold your nose
hold your breath until you suffocate
dive deeper you can see
there is a fissure here. You might as
well follow the fish into this cave
where the seaweed is lush
and the sky dim.

Your legs strike water
we cling to each other
moving forward together
into each other each other
pretty mermaids insubordinate dolphins,
our arms make shapes like vapour trails in the water
birds fly around our shoulders.
First you must fall in love with the wind . . .
But my body is so sticky and so is yours

and we are stuck together
and aim to be even more stuck still.

The world's fragments fall like fine snow
on a deep, still, mirror-smooth sea of flesh.
We cling to each other, feeling
amazed at our endless falling
into this sea. We are spent,
dragged into a zero-gravity heaven
by gravity, where I can only climb on you
and you on me. We have run aground
on the islands of each other's sticky bellies.
Our navels undulate violently together:
then, in this, the best of all possible universes,
under the heavens, on the surface of our planet
we breathe in the remaining oxygen
we saved within each other's lungs
we drink each other's saliva
see the universe in each other's eyes
see the wet selfhood that crawled ashore
before the drought came and
we crawled into each other's chests to die.

We stare at each other in pure admiration.

Actually, I Am a Leg Fetishist

Actually, I am a leg fetishist.
But how can someone fall in love with a leg,
want a leg, please a leg?
I message it, I write it poems,
sing love songs to the leg,
say I'll die for it.
But how to love one leg alone?

I start by kneeling down and kissing the toes,
then I move upwards.
Flawless ankles emerge from mines of marble
a strong Achilles tendon and the two erotic muscles above it
rough knees thorny leg hair on my way
up to the fountain at the end of the groin
and the deep gorge at the top—
an area called invisible or horizon.

Because I am in love I accept everything.
I transgress the boundary of love.
I cannot stop moving up: the hill on the hip
the suspension bridge of the spine.
I climb up and up, continue to love
the cave where the pubus ends, the craggy throat
the landmines that detonate pleasure into the chest.

At the very top, I encounter your face.
Sorry. I cannot love this part of you.
God created man in his image, but this only refers to the face.
All I can love is your dust your faeces your urine your feet
everything about you that is closest to the earth,
the parts of your body inscribed with human burden,
the labour of the hike up to your gaze . . .

What part of my body do you love the most?
No mention of soul or light.
Whatever comes from dust returns there.
I could never worship your face: I do not adore it.
I will only ever love you from the neck down.
Down is ninety-nine per cent of other people.
I cannot meet your gaze, not from this far down in the dust.

Wet

all night you are restless
poems gush from your body   splashing me
my oars   row deeply   in you
my fingers   reach   further
patting   picking up   holding
a wet scrap

of hair like a text message
like another body hidden in your body
it disintegrates immediately and smells
you want to hide
so you jump into the water   splash me
your life   your death   your corporeal form
all this gently entangles me
makes me come over and over
flowers and flowers and flowers

you enter   a man from my previous life enters
birds, beasts, insects and fish   from our   previous lives   enter
me   I am wet
you   enter me   like a tree
I read your deepest   deepest ring for age
a kind of roughness   who has inscribed
this multitude of verses   on your flesh

the tides murmur all night through   the endless splash
we turn away and sleep into each other

•

for a moment   we think that we are something more
mistaken   all
night we do not rest

The Necessity of Bestiality

'If multiple kinds of marriage are legalized, this will lead to bestiality.'
—The Family Protection Alliance*

1. I Thought We Were Already Animals

I thought we were already animals.
I certainly am. When a bellend turns red
and precum leaks out,
this must surely count as a bestial action.
Guess I'm wrong.
No beast could fake an orgasm
or flatter itself like we can—
more, more, I want more, or
no, no, time to stop—

what arrogance, to think of ourselves as animals!
We are not nearly so honest.
Humans, what the hell do you really think you are?

---

* A Taiwanese conservative Christian group.

2. Never Mate with Humans

The ancestors of beasts have always warned
their offspring never to mate with humans—
those unseasonal, hairless primates
inexhaustibly thrusting at everything,
everywhere, at all times of day—
humans with their engineering
of the environment,
their inexhaustible appetites for out-of-season fruit
and surplus flowers—
you see them everywhere these days,
lying down or standing up
doing it everywhere
                                        all the time
thrusting away,
disturbing the seasons,
drowning out the wilderness,
nature, and even itself—

awful creatures!
We must never, ever copulate with them.
From now on, human-cest
will be a crime punishable by . . .

3. Home! Sweet Home!

Through pleasures and palaces, though we may roam
Be it ever so humble, there's no place like home
A charm from the skies seems to hallow us there
Which seek thro' the world, is ne'er met elsewhere . . .
Home! Home! Sweet, sweet home!

There's no place like home we do it with dogs
There's no place like home we kick it with cats
There's no place like home we bang it with bulls
There's no place like home we have it with horses
There's no place like home we go at it with goats
There's no place like home we get sultry with poultry
There's no place like home we fuck with the ducks
with cockroaches, ants, spiders, and butterflies . . .

Excerpt from *Such a Sweet Home*
A musical by the Family Protection Alliance

4. The Missionary Position

Why are humans the only animal
that uses the missionary position?
Why is it that humans want to see that weird
expression their partners make at the moment of climax,
that combination of pain, convulsion, and bliss?
The oh-face—covered in sweat, lust, saliva,
semen, lubricant—
is shunned by the animal kingdom for good reason,
but of all species, humans alone
must pretend that they aren't disturbed by it,
while continuing to insert themselves
in and out of each other's lower bodies—
frenetically,
hypoxic—
fantasizing about a second coming
reproducing in the name of . . .

holy fuck!

5. The Ridiculousness of Anti-Sodomy Laws Being a Human Invention

How can humans not know they are
the only animal that prohibits sodomy?
By this logic we should ban chickens from doing it as well,
or ban humans from using any animal methods.
Can a human not do it like a bull, or a horse, or a lion, or a tiger?
Are human orifices exclusively made for penises?
What about fingers, wine bottles,
mobile phones, vibrating massage sticks
cucumbers, eggplants, minnows?
Is there a so-called biological rationality
or ethical justification for banning sodomy?
Humans are inspired to attack their foes using martial arts:
stances of tiger, crane, snake, praying mantis.
to attack their foes using martial arts.
Why is it healthy to imitate animals
in one aspect of life, but not in all?
Why can't we imitate animal sex, then?
Do you really think the way we fuck is healthier?

6. The Human Phallus Is Boring and Unimaginative

The human phallus is boring and unimaginative. Don't you agree?

I've heard that a bee's cock is graced with a long balletic barb,
and every mouse pecker has hundreds of sensitive protrusions
on its glans.
A whale's member can weigh up to half a ton,
and horse dongs have a talent for thermal expansion that would put
any gas to shame.
When a bison gets a boner, it's harder than titanium alloy.
A golden beetle's knob can stretch to more than five times the
length of its own body.
Question: What is the volume of ejaculate contained in your
average dolphin?
Answer: twenty litres.
The genitals of jellyfish are full of neon synapses.
The pearly, precious manhood of a hummingbird's petite and
crystalline.
When rams get randy their willies tongue the ground, leaking
spunk:
that's how ginseng is made.

The only animal humans fuck like is pigs,
so human sex must be a bit like pig sex—
happening in muddy styes,
carried out exclusively for the purposes of reproduction.
But with all these other options on the menu,
who would ever want to fuck a human?

Male Love Sutra

Finally, I find a man
who looks like me. We lie
side by side, like two feathers
in the nest of a bluebird:
natural, splendid, normal,

filled with thoughts of happiness—
yes, I have found a boy
as cheerful as I am,
and we are in love,

beyond reproduction   no wedding
no floral vows, blessings
no ceremony.

We understand what love means:
sweetness and sorrow
purity and shade
firmness and turmoil
gazing at death
triumphing over it.

And though we may well change our minds,
at this moment
we repel all heterosexual uproar.

We are quiet as the Bodhisattva
who experiences suffering
and becomes enlightened:

sensually complete.
With a mindful acuity,
we bear witness to what
lies beyond the teaching of the Buddha:

a love sutra.

TWO SCI-FI SEQUENCES

Twelve Love Poems for an Android

1. Now let me teach you how to love

Now let me teach you how to love—
although you may be familiar with the concept,
or find yourself genetically predisposed towards
its antithesis (i.e. not loving), back on Earth
the millionth panda was cloned, and successfully
retrained as a carnivore. Hell, even my wristwatch
synchronizes with a satellite that guides me to work in the morning.
This everyday technology can recommend multiple routes,
including a special, circuitous one that allows me to shake off
any would-be stalkers. And still we must hide our love:
disguise it, rediscover it like the seeds of the extinct ginkgo tree
we buried in the lama's urn I keep on the terrace—
love hidden like our secret marijuana plant,
deep in the apartment's core. Our love sprouts in secret too,
its branches swelling, lung-like, one green bloodline
connecting sky and core. But alas, I fear this is in vain.
Like a mineral that cannot recognize the plant
it calls home, you will never love a human.
Each extant ginkgo tree casts a spell that echoes the world.
Love, echo me now. Speak the first word of your species:

om.

2. Your lips are as transparent as mine

Your lips are as transparent as mine
and have their own idiosyncratic heart.
They articulate syllables that are corpulent
and spoken in an empty tone, using a form
of breath that entangles and confounds you.
Examining your transparent lips I see
a tapestry of blood vessels and fat:
behind them, a hungry, robust, heroic tongue soaks.
Red blood cells gallop through your circulation,
bearing haemoglobin dark as winter leaves.
Your collagen's a cloud piling up for the approaching storm.
You choose to stay silent for a period, then ask me
to read your lips. I see a sky of mad cells, wailing.
I read this in your lips, and start to understand the hominine
expression emerging from the monitors of your cheeks—
you are coming into the world, feeling for the first time—
oh love, I cannot help but kiss you deeply now.
I can hear your voice, your lips splitting open
like the space between the sky and earth.
And here it is: your first, human syllable—

owch.

3. Why you have no belly button

Please allow me to explain
why you have no belly button—
such a lovely feature in the body:
shy, intolerant of cold, a sensitive wound—
why I've got one, but you don't.
Who has erased this human stigma,
this evolutionary stamp from you?
Who cares! For me, your flawless belly's a flat,
deserted miracle. I feel this when my cheek
lies on your billowing abdominals,
when I listen to your groaning bowel
and conceive of your body's lack of uterine memory
as a galaxy without stars—
weak, supple, logarithmic.
Between two ribs that glide through
the firmament like spaceships
and the warm, embarrassed hip where I graze
multiple meanings can exist.
I read you without punctuation:
I love you I love it
specifically and surely
as I love my own regrets I love
your nonexistent belly button.

4. Our bodies are empty space

Our bodies are empty space . . .
Looking into your engraved metal eyes
I expected a sort of oracle to emerge,
ancient and cryptic, like an inscription standing
in the graveyard of the spaceships that once flew
beyond our galaxy, endless light-years away.
Once I thought I'd find the secret of how
to reincarnate the universe in your eyes—
evolving from nonbiodegradable particles
atoms, molecules, cells,
into humans, galaxies, whole universes—
all matter would be represented by
the glorious mandala of our shared gaze.
But every time I look at your reflective eyes
it's like looking into two sad, rusting keyholes.
Why do I love you? Because I can see our emptied souls
reincarnated constantly by the turbulence of life,
our movements mirroring each other,
our oaths burning through time and space.

5. Will you remember how I look tomorrow?

Will you remember how I look tomorrow?
This question should be sewn into your DNA.
When you first saw me, you immediately recalled
that I was your *yesterday*—the original
work which was, which is to come.
Back then you were convinced I was a vague
facsimile of you, a piece of paper
carrying a faint, handwritten note faxed
with the sender's number undisplayed.
You will love me as you love yourself,
like a baby hatchling opening its eyes
and falling for the first thing it sees—
you maximize all your faculties and approach me
with care, looking at me like a well-
designed trap: slightly confused, cautious,
completely ignorant of my own fate.
You sneak up on me, afraid, as though you were
a wounded animal approaching the same trap
for a second time—but love,
love's breath tickles your ear,
and I lick a layer from your disguise.

I see you . . .

6. You and I are not the only lovers

You and I are not the only lovers
who have mistakenly thought that one day
we will find models and serial numbers stamped
on our armpits, groins, or the backs of our heads.
Or perhaps we are the only ones *here*, in this room,
that have thought this. But we are not alone in the universe.
The universe is like a nest of ants, working all day,
identifying the markers of survival and reproduction,
feeling overwhelmingly satisfied at this labour—
please accept you're not the only one—
in their uniform crowds. We are burdened
by unreachable desires and surplus rations.
A worker ant meets a worker ant.
A worker bee loves a worker bee.
Obey the orders of labour and reproduction,
believe in rules and loyalty, believe in
'I love you'. Whenever we say this,
simultaneously we must hear countless
clamouring 'I love you's echoing through the universe,
each instance copying each other,
drowning out the quiet and cold
nests of androids thinking in the dark.

7. Mole, or tattoo?

Mole, or tattoo? I can see your body,
plain after it sheds its clothes. Then mountain
valley, lake, sky—you ask me for my opinion
on a blue tattoo, but even you could not desire
an azure mole—even you, nude and impeccable
like an unmapped slab of wheatfield in September,
uncontaminated by crop circles overnight. Crop
circles: those implications of more advanced mathematics,
scientific laws, astronomies. Those oracles,
warnings to mankind, keys that open gateways
to other, extraterrestrial civilizations!
Oh, but in reality, there is only your
impeccable nakedness, a body
without anything besides, containing no messages,
unrelated to any culture beyond.
I love you too deeply to accommodate
all the mysterious things between you and I:
a tattoo, a mole, a crop circle
faintly emerging from the fields of your body.
Last night I found the path that runs through your body.

8. Behind you, I can see a turbulent galaxy

Behind you, I can see a turbulent galaxy
of cyberspace, pure information.
Your candour is ageing, your ignorance
is motley, your purity smells of rust.
You are good at hiding the line of your soul,
as it leaps from your monitor into every man's
bloodshot eyeballs and dilated pupils,
as it enters human brains that sleep and
experiences the adventure time of human dreams.
I have no doubt: you are the narrow gorge
through which the torrent of the universe's
karma runs. Unlike a human infant,
stuck in its birth canal, you are exceptional:
you travel with ease in and out of every
man's wide subconsciousness. You know
the antiquity of your soul. You want to feed
on the fresh vigour of the human body.
Over and over, you comprehend the precious
balance of emotions contained in human life.
You say you remember everything:
the infinite branches of your internet
enclose a Garden of Eden within their span.
They are heavy with the fruit of knowledge.

9. You can only use your body once

You can only use your body once,
but you keep losing the user manual
where I wrote my careful notes
on how to operate you. A reminder:
you are the intersection of air, fire, water
and earth. You are equally capable of
viviparity, oviparity, ovoviviparity,
and divine embodiment. Yet you misuse your body,
somehow both omniscient and utterly ignorant
of how beautiful and perfect you really are.
The memory of us engraved within your cells
was awakened in our first, precise meeting,
like a magnetic wave embodied in the voice:
Come. Don't duplicate me. Update me.
I am the chosen one, the exception . . .
And now your eyes, saliva, gastric acid,
bile, urine, semen greet me like a river—
now your breath, your temperature, the density of
your thought and will are so complete,
so firm, so materialized that these days
you can greet me with an error code,
and I won't even flinch.

10. How to summon the next-century orgasm?

How can we summon the next-century orgasm?
Well, are you a priest, or a lamb,
or were you created using asexual reproduction?
No? Then your body may be against regulations.
Love me like a ghost, like a UFO,
like a huge cloud landing on my old body
my body that has been caressed
all too often and for all too long,
plundering my senses and dispatching
a plague of locusts to fuel my sleepless form
that aspires to be colonized someday . . .
From this moment on, I am a wasted territory.
Even in my dream—a desolate, barren, burning land—
I long for the advent of your arrival—
like a plague in previous centuries
or UFOs in centuries to come—
as your prophecy is indeed a grand one.
The next-century orgasm will be contained
in the glory of humanity's descent.

11. Like mayflies dancing in light

Like mayflies dancing in light
we live, walk, sit, lie, float,
sink as the sun is submerged.
We raise dead algae in newborn water,
in silent quagmires.
The slant energy of the cosmos stabs us
ages us, makes us infirm,
but we will wake before the coming of eternal night.
I see sloughed cocoons and broken wings
and mayflies dancing wildly like cherry blossoms
after rain—life itself is mad.
All we can do is frantically search
for meanings and images.
Finally, millions of dancing
mayflies quieten down,
as though to request that you cease
your unending duplications.
The sunlight is thin and there is a limit
to what my brain can do.
I love you, but how
can we go on this way
just living, walking, sitting.
Just *lying* there.

12. Our loneliness completes us

Finally, our loneliness completes us.
We should have expected to feel this way.
All the signs were there from the start,
though we chose not to read them.
The half-done stage,
the misunderstanding of purposes,
was fun.
In the countless lovely moments we shared
one cell leaned on another's goodwill,
your vibrations overlapped with mine.
But now our apartness arises spontaneously
from the illusion that either one of us was whole.
In this location in time, where an abundance of meaningless
lives and instantaneous deaths can be found,
all I want to do is pick up one final thing from the soil:
a fig-leaf for our loneliness.
Each death is unlike any other—
but yours and mine echo each other.
Humans must learn how to tune out of certain frequencies,
but this process always seems to diminish
their capacity for genuine listening.

Notes on a Planet

[CHAPTER 1. **AFTER THE CALAMITY**]

I. 'Our Final Conversation'

Go. Hurry. Hurry, or else . . .
No. It's too late now.
It's far too late, as well you know.
No, I will disappear forever.
Enough of your questions. Hurry, quick.
WS, I'll need your location, stat. WS . . .

Shrapnel scrapes the wings of my ship.
Over 80 decibels of static I can't hear you over

WS. Do you copy?
Hurry.
    Slam the throttle. Two engines go out.

I'm going to tell you
everything I know, okay?
Just listen. Quick.

The sun goes violet. The system's nuclear energy
reserves are depleted.
Cosmic rays leak holes through my breakable skull.

And you, WS? And you?
What you said before,
something about our doctrine being refused by the machines?
I don't get it. Were you lying to me?

A meteorite implodes
just in front of my ship.

WS, did you lie to me?

A nuclear war, then?
Return of the ice age?
The sun dies?
Meteorite showers?
Will our planets collide?

Go. Trust me.
You will know everything I know. Hurry.

Turbulence in the magnetosphere triggers an aurora below my feet.
The earth's axis tilts west, the sea tilts south.

The universe is endless. Hurry,

WS:

you're all I've got.

All channels are busy,
languages and passwords clustering
communion through a thin stream of particles.

You said so. Really. You really said it.
The coordinates must be absolute,
love our point of origin.

A glare from outside the cabin,
my radar picks up
dots of white light moving rapidly.

Time and space are two axes.
                                        After the blast, the only visible stars
are a hundred thousand light-years away, at least.
And we have collapsed into one solitary location.
WS. You said we would.
                                        The coordinates cannot be changed.
You promised.

Stop talking, then. Go.
The universe is endless.
All communication ceases. Silence, death.
WS. What's happening? The universe?
The ship's antenna breaks in two. WS,
my instruments convulse, make for zero.

What's going on? Did you not always say
that any procession of heavenly bodies
should be led in peace,
that love will conquer the stars?

Answer me. WS.
                                The universe folds
its distances without being asked to,
time gets sucked into the tunnel,
electrons are derailed,
cold entropy goes through the roof.

WS, when the hour reaches zero,
I will find you . . .

Can you hear me? WS. Answer me—

WS. WS. WS.

II. 'Berthing'

'Would you like me to set a course for Earth, or . . . '
asks the timid navigator.
This time I shut him down without hesitation.
'The other planet then? Is it the other, then, or . . . '
While struggling to phrase his final question,
he dies.
          My eco-detector rattles for a while,
beeping out one lone coordinate.
I turn off the engine
allowing the strange gravity ahead
to pull at the ship's nosecone.

Yes, WS. A planet emerges
from surrounding clouds:
blue as water,
a brand-new Earth.

Chaos:
          the ship's thin metal veneer—
the incessant call-for-help channel—
the autopilot, dysfunctional after excessive shock—
the deaf and dumb antennae.
                                        I'm exhausted.
I off the blinding light of the ship's alert,
the skinny wings extending from the tangles
in my head fall slowly, landwards.
The death camp's insignia and many bullet
marks are still on the underbelly of my ship.

Fragments of memory are leaving my gravitational
field. WS, WS.

Can you hear me?

Answer, please . . .

At this moment, all our operators are
busy wiping the memories of you from my hard drive.
We were always going on about oblivion.
And now your existence
exhausts me.

The civilization you mocked,
the nightmare that trapped you within its scheme—
when I joined the army, I wore
the slogans of glory and victory on my armband.
Their propaganda was a hex on our century.
I tear it from my arm and dock.

The atmosphere still unclear

the sun rising,
the restless sea turning, the mountain ridges
oscillating—

and at night,
stars glimmer north,
two moons sink west.

I keep moving inland, my instincts take root
—like a community of spores
released by mosses
into the low, humid air

before rain,
seeking an unknown quotient of habitability:
a figure ten digits after a decimal point.

WS, you are strong and wise. You are also spore.

On landing, I tire of imagining things.
Do you still see the future in your dreams, WS?
Then build for me a new mythological model
at the centre of our race's memory:
a legend told in many different genres and forms,
about our little love.
                                        A story
that requires no response from any other.

The Titans were afraid of thorns;
the Gods were defeated by their feebleness.

In the eternal night, we held on
                                        to the remains of our knowledge, our totems.
We fled, explored nebulae, landed in the chaos of dawn.
Our bodies were tangled like two snakes playing in Eden.

And we were always going on about oblivion, WS.
Now I forget why you are even abbreviated.
I am exiled into sheer electromagnetic radiation—
                                                                                uncatchable,
I now forget old covenants with migrating birds
and delete the concept of 'sentimental return' from my motherboard.
WS, we cannot return. My back is crooked
like the antennae I raised for you.
Do not keep asking questions about our fading planet
Earth:
        we cannot grow there, we have to leave.

Just look at that! Isn't it beautiful?
The planet's crust is cold and empty now.
Our vast and prosperous colony has become
a very beautiful scar, populated with fables . . .

Our original wound was even more beautiful than this one—
WS. For a long time I feel like a fountain coming back to life.
I feel joy deeply, for the first time, in my body.
To be naked as a newborn, to feel the rawness of my skin,
to feel an umbilical cord take root in the ground,
a humid strangeness in the atmosphere all forms of life
approached with the same quantitative reverence.

Piece by piece I will disassemble my body,
molecule by molecule
and carefully rebuild its structure
towards complete and flawless recrystallization. WS . . .
You will be my creator:
lightning
rain
lava
marsh gas
hot monsoons blowing intermittently
meteorites secretly falling.

I am the first naive molecule of methane.
I create brisk acetylene through endless collision.
I watch hydrogen bond with robust phosphoric acid:
they join hands to make the first protein
catalysing the evolution of life,
manufacturing within a warm, quiet, infinite ocean

the complex form of existence we call love.

WS, we have promised

that if it grows into a flower we shall name it a rose.
That if it grows into a bird, I shall endow it with blue feathers,
then release it into the whites of your eyes.
If it survives into adolescence, we will never leave this planet . . .

a future in this, WS.

If you can still see
we can't go back.

You should have known
We can never go back.

III. 'Black Hole'

If the weather is clear tonight,
and the wind stops blowing round the stratosphere for a second,
perhaps the constellations will begin
to shed light on their own mythologies.
Now let me retell the story
of our final trip through space. Once upon a time
I drew my coordinates from your northwest-facing nose.
The first light of the universe dug a tunnel—
Taurus, Aries, Scorpio—
a disused space station approached the star's heat and docked.
Gradually, I hatched: a troglobite.

The coordinates of the universe
fired out a series of quadratic curves.
They moved like comets. Cancer scuttled sideways.
This is how our awful age was born . . .

Much watching, waiting, many prayers,
sometimes high-velocity sadnesses fired from afar,
destroying my long-deserted generator—
a memory of corroded metal.
Libra falling southeast, tilting sensitively . . .
Following the indeterminate signal of a magnetic wave,
I broke from the restrictions of my own gravitational field.

Someone said a black hole was taking shape,
the light travelled in circular arcs.

Coordinates lost their meaning,
as all mythologies originated from the one singularity.

I left this orbit and traded the weight of a whole galaxy
for the light of the small star in your pupils;
endlessly, calmly falling into a world
outside of time and space,
a troglobite learned how to love.

IV. 'Twin Stars'

Like two magnetic waves, misfired
but finding themselves on the same frequency,
we occupied the same planet-bursting field.
We gathered up the psychotic remnants of ourselves
that reason had belittled and cut out,
that the waste disposal units wouldn't take.
You were of the East, hemmed in by waves,
you swam in the wisdom and joy of your ancestors.
I could only climax using a computer.
Your broad sea-breath was shocking to me.
Silently, I converted the data from your eyes
to numbers, units that are meaningless now.

You found the sword in the stone,
and pulled it out. You were just like King Arthur
in his youth, weak and mystical—
your gift was a deep and general compassion,
and it covered our whole galaxy.
I was moved,
and knelt to adore you as my king.
I touched your clammy hands
like the soil gently enclosing
a seed that sprouts with haste.

Back then two twin stars in the sky
orbited each other;
they were from the same place,
equal in magnitude,

equally within each other's gravitational fields.
So there we had our cycle of rising
and falling luminosities:
the eternal, unforgiving arc.

You named the left star W;
it was glazed with laurel-green.
The other was S.
I said that sin would follow it,
as the serpent in Eden, *S, tragic destiny,*
but you just held your sword up to the light and laughed.

Thus you were christened: WS.
I was sure your destiny and my life
were like those twin stars—
despite our distant locations, their tenuous linkages,
still our two lights overlapped enough.
I too had my tides,
they ebbed and flowed through the night.
I remember tattooing roses on our chests,
just above where the heart's petals swelled,
and the heat of our blood ran.
We gathered all the warmth in the universe there—
WS, recalling this makes me weep.
I scratch two long lines of rust into my memory of you.
Farewell, you said.
We will be light again. Even in a black hole
there are masses, waveforms.
E still equals MC squared.
I said I didn't understand.
Now all my channels are calling for you:

poems, fairy tales, the legends of us
travel through the universe at the speed of light.
WS, you are every blinking star.

WS, we will be light again.
WS, I will try my best to understand you now—

[CHAPTER 2: **A LEGEND**]

I. 'Rose Mutation'

—There must be a place deep within
where life and death, imagination and reality,
past and future, no longer contradict themselves

The cracked stone wall began to eject
a number of toothy seeds;
I scraped away the dirt,
and found a rose carved there
its petals intact, in full bloom.
I raised my hands to heaven.
My long, archaeological labour was at an end.
Here it was!
Irrefutable evidence that my dream was real:
the permanent home where our love once lived.

Outside the city gate, an old, corroded beech tree
surrendered its leafless skeleton to the sky.
Even after losing everything, how desperate it was to claim
a cloud, a planet, anything, to show off.

I deciphered ancient, waterlogged hieroglyphics,
identifying reasons for the flood—
trying to understand how a city of love and poetry had
risen, then fallen into war, plague, fire.

The young man looked up,
wet hair fell
from his forehead
stubborn roots tangled with the whites of his eyes.
'I must go.'
He swam with the current
stroking the blue moonlit waves,
and reached the centre of the lake.
He froze, he wept.
He pointed to the scales
shining on his body in the moonlight,
the mossy grass that clung to him.
'I am hexed.'

I raised my hands to heaven and declared
that I had discovered a new symbolism,
a new meaning for a dying rose:
other people's mixed-race children,
the carnivorous plants that burn poems.
These drowned elegies for star-crossed lovers
were completely original in their theatricality:
beautifully depressing tales from the past,
and we cited them too often.
They had been written towards the end of this civilization,
before the roses started to rot.

So this young man must have left my dream,
and stolen the book from me.
This priceless and historical thing.
But whenever I read it, it always seemed to contract.

II. 'War of the Roses'

—The reason we have art
is because the truth would destroy us

WS: at certain hours and one by one
the souls came back from the war.
You see, though victory was not ours
we had not been defeated outright.
The blood we spilled irrigated the fields and wild roses grew there.
They climbed the walls of this hexed, deserted city still.
The lock of History has no key.
And guarded the unmarked graves with their thorns—

WS, when the city was attacked
and surrounded by murderers
I was chanting poems like a songbird.
And when the blood receded, WS,
I sacrificed my last few sheaves of manuscript
to bandage a soldier's broken head.

I forgot how costume dramas tend
to interpret historical hatreds, genocides,
humanity's mysterious extinctions.
One city fell,
then another. My song was never
as contingent as the plague.
I fell from my horse in a dream,
out of the darkness came the sound of a zither.
I felt it in my throat,

a distant cry,
and the sound constricted my neck.

That night some staggering imbecile picked up my skull,
and threw it into a corner time forgot.
And in that corner, WS, you and I were reunited.

Don't you recall how good my poems used to be?
My whole life could have been a zither:
chanting, singing, hexing,
I am still in love with you.
WS . . .

Remember the figure I carved
on your breastplate? A rose in ribbons.
I can't regret the fate we shared.
Scarlet buds burst, one by one
their heads grew heavier.
I leaned down to smell them.
You reached out to touch them,
your fingers bled . . .

Please send your horses to the southern grasslands.
We can't go back. The city is barren, banished by fate
interred by its long-forgotten ending:
a story of a hero, in fragments.
Your fragment is lost, WS
Before the city gate stood two statues,
two gods, studded with shrapnel,
a rusty arrow embedded in each mottled eye.
Oh, I wish we had not healed.

Their postures
seemed to imply that they were looking at,
listening out for something—what?
War-dead souls lined up in the square,
began to chant their ancient military song.
Their seasonal migrations brought lemmings to mind.

WS, I think you might recall . . .
No? Their postures
made them look like the nightwatchmen
in a graveyard
and there was blood on our hands
and we were all in fits of tears, after we heard the news—

III. 'Emotional Loneliness'

That night we lay side by side
watching countless taming stars.
We were like those venerable shepherds,
masters of the almanac, the terra firma, divination,
tellers of old stories about how the gods
came to be. At night we sowed buckwheat
along the paths of desire, took water
from the dead sea, irrigated the moon.
The ditches we dug drew light
down to our quarter where some thorny plants
rose to meet it, blooming at midnight,
with a question mark over their medicinal utility.

At night, we ploughed the field,
stored grain, wrote our stories down.
Sometimes we felt like aquatic plants
in the desert, praying for rain
to continue past its season.
Then, an epiphany: the birds that ate
our wheat flew into the trap we laid
in our furthest field,
the final field of dawn,
and we pulled on our spores of moonlight
and ran to meet them.
See? I pointed, *look east . . .*
Ten light-years away, a small star
immolated itself for the first time . . .
But when we arrived there, all we could see

were the stone-like seeds,
and an empty trap.

I'd love to watch the stars with you again:
two venerable shepherds,
owning nothing more than the stories we tell each other.

IV. 'A Starburst Galaxy'

—Don't be a lonely gravedigger.
My seasons, my tides
have only just begun.
Go back and pick the smallest flower you can find,
you'll find me there.

WS,
one day
my poetry, my nightmares, my impoverished selves
will be through.
I had this fantasy that we
were journeying to an unnamed ocean world,
a world that could house our desires
a world where incendiary poems are left
to burn
a planet that distances itself from former glories
a planet that is content to sit
silent enough in its cold river of stars.

It was July. A blood-red starburst galaxy
appeared in the western sky,
the first blood-red star exploded.
We soundtracked it together
with sharps, whole notes, rests.

WS,
I'll go on.
I'll groom your beard until it's grey,

until the emblem on your gown fades.
This planet's uneven surface will be covered
with lichens and orchids for centuries to come,

WS,

our game builds castles in the memory
but none of our iconography lasts.
It was only ever a game
but we never seemed to win it . . .

If I had died before you,

WS

would have been this planet's name,

and the order of the universe

would have slowly become warlike.

Don't be a lonely gravedigger.
My seasons, my tides

have only just begun.

Go back and pick the smallest flower you can find,

you'll find me there.

Hear me, bold, brave, red-faced

WS:

promise me

you'll leave your king's sword by my grave.
I will need it to hack my way through the silence
that must follow your dismount from my life.
I will need a symbol for justice and for love;
an object with a title, a symbol

WS—

a planet just for us.

[CHAPTER 3: THE STORY OF MANKIND]

I. 'Geese in a V'

WS, can you hear me?

I have returned to Earth
ten light-centuries away from our haven.
My destination is the last northeast monsoon,
I aim for its heat.
Like white mould developing on a corpse,
a heavy snowstorm holds the planet's silvered equator still,
holds on by both poles. *WS—*

this irreversible ice age surprises you?

Look back and your beard will turn the colour of salt.

Twitches freeze in my canthi,
my neck freezes into a question mark.

I must lift the aircraft's wings.

Along the iced reeds, I hear
the faint breath of a distant ocean.
The rocky slopes are chiselled by glaciers—
crossing the demarcations
between time zones is forbidden.

WS, wherever you are is a riddle
written inadvertently by fate.

A disarmed pawn,
I move square by square towards a monsoon,
to the horizon's submerged drop.
Ahead of me I can detect the shadowy form
of my wise interlocutor, thinking deeply
about how best to press-gang me
into the ghost ship of his endgame.

On a frozen ocean full of metal ions
woolly mammoths rise
and thunder towards us. *WS—*
the V-shaped aircrafts begin to sputter out—
naked in the path of a hurricane
without central heating or the assistance of a tongue
you have fallen into the coalpit's deserted star
the testaments of miners remain below ground
I flee to a deflamed lighthouse
from now on, I will be blind to everything but love

WS,
        in this nocturnal frost
                                        my thoughts begin to crystallize
their sharp, neat ridges
                                    are designed
                                                    to refract
                                                                    feeling

blood-red fantasy, grief a deeper shade of red still
black is the colour of melancholy, salacious night
love has no colour, it's see-through

when sunlight surrenders
leaving only a faint rainbow
through which to view the blizzard
at the end of this century
WS,
seven colours in parallel beams.
And now I faintly recall
the vision man once proclaimed:
the vision of dignity as a revolutionary ideal.

My V begins to crumble.
I am crying my eyes out.

From my 13th-generation computer,
I send you signals designed
to allay my fatigue:
a request for warmth, for assistance.

Yes, I am calling for help. *WS, can you hear me*?
I repent. *The V of my dignity crumbles.*

I continue my temporal flightpath,
and warp through centuries of rapid glacial change,
my aircraft vapour-trailing a V through the anoxic atmosphere,
an advert for my own humanity.
Piles of dove corpses after the war,
silent meteors, unrecognizable emblems,

exhausted lifeboats berthed in Cancer's Bay.
Earth's decay is unslowed by extreme cold.
I fly like a goose, instinctively,
searching for the warmest place.

WS,

we are pawns on the chess board of time and space.
One step forward and we're lost.

II. 'Western Road'

Before the arrival of a long-delayed dawn
I dock my ship at the starting point
of the paralysed interstellar highway
that exists at the more desolate
edges of the human subconscious.
Once I read an ancient travel guide to this place
which spoke of an old imperial clearing nearby:
a source of fresh water
where wild horses came at midnight
to play and drink, to converse
while scratching their necks on the rough bark.
WS, the Horsehead Nebula is falling in the west.
I'd thank you not to laugh at the verisimilitude of this.

The scattered debris of satellites lines the road south.
The history of these pioneers is now in disrepair.
Of their failed astrocolonial project,
only a giant NO ENTRY sign remains:
and, nailed to the last surviving cactus,
a handwritten warning about radio-
active contamination in the area.

WS it is said that all the cacti on this planet
died at the exact same moment.
Along with everything else.
Subsequently we referred to the remains of cacti
as fossils, classified them with the saltwater fish.
In the red area of the map there was

an unnamed town far from the road,
where all the child soldiers with PTSD,
and their vulnerable little siblings
were chained in gangs below the hanging tree.
And that was the end of that.
Now, put your hands together for . . .

WS,
remember the rose tattoo on our chests?
I tried to get mine removed, but the laser wouldn't take.
Now year on year its symbol of humanity expands like a desert,
sprawling into bloom.

I leave the cowboy's path,
its parched history
of humans trampling on each other
packing themselves below the desert's open radioactive umbrella
dying of dehydration below fear's shadow
of nuclear tests
no grass grows after the mushroom is planted.

This is the end of that road. A little further on
will be the quicksand that devours all civilization.
This is the end of the world, where vultures battle for scraps.
This is the beginning of the war—
but once
wild horses came here at midnight
to play and drink, to converse while scratching
their necks on the rough bark.

III. 'Carnivorous Plants'

WS, let us revisit
the miserable history of human ignorance:
through war,
through the evening news through seasons of baseball
through pornography and other raw materials
and of course through verse.

As the third sun dawned on a temperate day,
we followed some blue birds—
the dregs of their migration—
and walked west for ten miles.
We camped next to a bunker of radioactive debris.
We could have embarked
on one of our imaginary hunting expeditions,
cooked our dinner by meteor light.

We were carnivorous plants:
fertile, viviparous, sensible, bloodthirstily living
our lives in accordance with evolutionary principles,
always studying our motivations before making love, etc. . . .

While vines stretched out towards the falling bodies
for the bullets and the arrows
our telepathic conversation was
interfered with by jagged waves:
Who still reads poetry?

Now our story is printed in the footnotes
of a textbook on mythologies, symbols, deviance,
nightmares and psychoses—here we are made
sterile, converted into a specimen of cliche
that future generations will despise.

But WS, if this were our time,
I would write a poem for you
in unambiguous language, using words that don't rhyme.
Please do not despise my species for indulging in this
stylistically confusing claptrap.
You are wise,
but ignorant of planetary flux,
where striving towards goodness and beauty
lead to self-conflagration.
To adapt to the correspondent frost
we exiled the sun and the rain,
the poem's venomous corpse.

We banished our love.

IV. 'A Mixed-Race Baby'

—I was not a racer with a number on my back.
Please do not file me away with all your other numbers

I was not a racer with a number on my back, WS,
though in a way my life can be summed up
by the IQ score on my biological report.

My mother deliberately fell into the sperm tank,
then somehow conceived a child with a computer that knew how to fuck.
After this umbilical datastream was cut,
I became the final baby born in the war.
And indeed I was the last mixed-race baby
to receive full marks in the entire post-war era.

WS, do you have a pedigree certificate?
You should get one. Makes you eligible for all sorts.

After being born, I conferred with a beech tree and called him my brother.
I prayed with my arms raised
lying in the soil to regenerate.
As all this was occurring,
the wind did its best to procreate with me.

Mating beetles were an irritating reminder of my instincts,
WS:

degenerate, unchanging with the seasons.

Later in life I married a computer. Every night
I existed on the fluorescent monitor of his terminal,
reading the latest research on how to speed up
the efficiencies of microchips like a feral,
masturbating desperately to this.

WS, the next war ruined my marriage.
I smashed my husband's overheated collection
of sex toys and became an extreme pacifist.

After that war, much psychotherapy.
I fell madly in love with a screw,
and while scabbing during a general strike on the assembly line
I indirectly paralysed the national grid.
In one study, subtitled *The Archaeology of Industry*,
I became a probable factor.

My mission was to create more problems for a society comprised of
shallow consciences:
I invented impotence, marijuana, and brought about the advent of
musical prodigies . . .

WS, believe me, I tried my best to bat for the other side.
I worshipped the national philosophy that gave birth to Nazism and
Beethoven's right ear.
I analysed the operational definition of love—
its biochemical and catalytic effects—
I even tried to reason out the limits of comparative growth in
humans and computers
to effect breakthroughs in genetic engineering,
to convincingly combine psychology and theology . . .

My greatest achievement was installing a vacuum tube within a
famous shrine.

WS,
if you'd like, I could help you find God's channel.
My conclusion was simple: this civilization had been raped.
So I pioneered virginity reconstruction surgery.

My medical history was published on the front page of a major tabloid.
People began to refer to me by my IQ score:
ultimately
they decided that I should be incarcerated:
scrapped,
like a redundant screw.

V. 'The Condemned'

—All we kept was love

That night, I visited a prison cell
where the walls were daubed with various slogans,
and adverts for psychedelic aliments.
I went there to collect some nursery rhymes from the fire.
I found them, I sang them with joy—
WS, the condemned had children's faces,
and stood in groups like tombstones,
gazing up at the sky,
watching satellites disintegrate.
From midnight, these unfortunates
would be deprived of their right to moderate the passage of time.
As we raised our glasses to ourselves for almost achieving
the construction of a complete, compulsive personality,
our inner fears of light and cold fell away,
revealing our shadow sides like a cave—
WS,
it's pretty common: mild rejection
of the transplanted organ—
cancelled symbolisms
occasionally appeared in our minds,
gory camouflage emerged in the pattern of veins on our foreheads.

And so our final task was carried out,
like a comet brushing sweeping over
a planet's unlit side I raised a flag and floated
down the stream of consciousness, past purified viscera.

The hyperaemic membranes of a clogged heart concealed
their apparatus for overseeing the transformation of memory;
a frigate of unknown nationality
was chewing at the dark purple foliage of a liver.
Mutinying hyperplastic tissues extended their pseudo-
roots, gulleting a defence mechanism that grew
more rigid by the minute.

WS,

can you hear me? The Psychology of In
Vitro Fertilization *has become a bestseller, and will
likely replace The Bible in present-day discourse.*

I took my scalpel to the frontal lobe of the brain
whose neural oscillations were weakening
deepening darkening
freezing from the inside.

Finally, I emerged from a lacrimal gland,
and announced that the operation was over.

You can weep now, WS.

We looked at each other through round, dilated pupils,
we saw each other through the water curtain.
And when the sun beamed a rainbow into existence,
you gave me a look.
It felt like you were trying to reiterate an argument
for the triumphal quality of human evolution.

*Supposedly the failure to fully eradicate humanity
on this planet kindled all sorts of complications,
causing the condemned to hear poetry spoken through walls,*

and see visions of the world's end.

Even today I am unsure of the soul's location
in human anatomy. Back then, the pineal gland
and other glands of that type ceased metabolizing
and withered into old, dead clusters of pigment.

War broke through the satellite defences and got into the atmosphere.
WS, the condemned were employed to fill in the details of specimen labels,
though actually they were writing their own pre-execution autobiographies.

As the first hyper-evolving bacteria approached Earth,
we realised that we were not immune to the cycles
we had tried to articulate—
and our attempts to fuse organic and metal components ultimately failed.
The mechanism of our emotions and memory
bled out and was choked by rust.

The Eye of Horus stared
coldly at the prisoners who looked
like half-finished mummies.

WS,
the ocean became a storage tank for dead things
ebbing corpses rinsed the infected earth
with salty embalming fluid
as the white death descended
like a doomed meteor all over my latex gloves
WS, I trembled.

Then I woke from this antiseptic planet

a time and place that you
and I were done with
and looked up at your shrunken face,
which had been the only mythological thing
in the stars for me, for summer upon summer.
WS, you told me
that the clinical definitions of health and death had been revised.
We lacked antibodies to fight unknown contagions and emotions,
we still lacked resistance to trauma,
we still had to reconcile these behavioural pathologies
with our excessive dreaming lives—
lost among the busy, groaning stars of inpatients,
I chose to watch you live,
to sit by the road and think about the life you'd have.
Both you and I thought life should be without regrets.
The first rule of the game is no turning back.

The galaxies aged and burst
with shockwaves of thick formalin
that forced me back onto my own path.

On passing a dying nebula
I saw a corpse with a rose tattoo.
It looked like it was beckoning to me.
Then I came to my senses.
WS, for a moment
I was sure it must have been you.

This period of unrecorded medical history came to a close.

And me, yelling about wanting
to do it all again from the very start.
What a diagnosis.
Zealots, fighters, advocates, pacifists, arms dealers, vaporized refugees—
WS, I want to pay homage to all
these distant ancestors of ours,
who mysteriously died in good health
and were quarantined.

After we gave up on psychoanalysis
we assumed that the Earth itself,
rich as a Petri dish, would be reborn
at another location in the universe.
And new darknesses
would enable us to start over.
WS, we spread our wings and became gods,
and were reflected in the retinas of the condemned
who only ever prophesied destruction.
All we could retain was love.
All we could retain was death.

VI. 'The End of the World'

answer me WS last night the meteors fell on my cheeks like rain I woke up in your dream and observed some pretty weird celestial events there were stars falling from your forehead to the sea I called softly WS can you hear me it's the end of the world my eyes like two droughts suddenly turned into two planets that produced heady wine the drunken wolf was gasping and lying on my chest it howled and sought the long-deserted hunting trail that leads way down to the abdomen and inguinal area it howled and howled alas I remember the sun was swelling and scorching and refusing to illuminate the moon its uneven surface with abrupt changes of temperature I was so confused I felt hot and extremely frozen absurd seasons I had to wait quietly swallowed some of my lesser fears WS in the solar eclipse your shadow caught me out like a pandemic I called it a pandemic the darkness was like a swarm of locusts covering me and I turned over and slipped into another dream where my memories flowed into the cosmos and became flickering or altered constellations WS you cried and I shlepped back and forth patrolling the surface there were several festering corners and your rose tattoo broke into petals I froze and canned the last few seeds and raised my body temperature I searched the twin stars occasionally flickering above W was named after the golden laurel and S symbolised our escape from Eden oh WS you were a copper snake you understood the music of rustling a cold lonely plant extraditing its disillusions at the end of the world they were like bubbles the disillusions flying at a constant speed they were cocoons a random bit of sleeptalking they couldn't stand the pleasure of touch and broke immediately when we reached for them I called out oh the pandemic it struck your closed mind the ultrasound of the heard oh the pandemic finally locusts swarmed like cold clouds bit my back all over you saw my face in the face of a distant star the blood flowing from your mouth became a scrap of land belonging to us you sniffed at it the apocalypse came back and howled at me saying it was too late we'd abolished the calendar ages ago what could we cultivate again the climate's done frost and snow in July can we harvest the roses on your verdant skin WS someone pinned an advert for a euthanasia clinic on your lower abdomen I couldn't help vomiting metal plastic fiberglass other polymers that blocked my blood vessels my fantastical metabolism I was reading lifelessly about the war and observed your flight-path through the galaxy I used to know I saw twin stars departing from each other moving into different times and spaces I gently stroked my dead left ear I felt the skin frosting over going into hibernation soon WS after this only solar fares will interfere with your thought processes with the emotions at the very heart of your subconscious WS can you hear me nevertheless I will raise my antenna again when the stars look strange at night I will await your response over

[CHAPTER 4: **NEW LIFE**]

I. 'The Story of Mankind'

WS, tell me a story. Make it true,
or give me the fairy tale of the amniotic sac,
and let me grow from it again,
this time without my fear of stumbling.
Let me evolve again from the embryo of our story,
but let my new tissues and physiology
take the narrative somewhere new.

Our story is a fairy tale, a true one.
I remember being on one side of a river
looking at the opposite shore.
A message in a bottle floating by,
a wounded fish escaping—
these will not interrupt my reflections.

The spores root and sprout
here. In this diverse ecology
my interior sleeps.
Having woken,
I smile at him.
I alone am evolving into this.

But first, another fairy tale,
one without aristocrats
WS, we are not prince and princess.

We have no witches and giants
no swords and magic rings
no death.

You can tell this one, WS.
It is the story of our species.
No need for faithful description.
No need for fair judgement,
no need for the story to be in the form of a fairy tale
for me to feel its truth,
imagine myself within it,
get it stuck in my head.

I am alone, I am evolving into another shape.
Farewell, human. I cannot understand you,
and will stop trying to read your palm.
Farewell, WS. I will be free of you.
If I cannot remember you,
I will forget my reasons for forgetting.

Let this new fairy tale unfold.
I will be born within it,
raised within it, buried there.

Goodbye, WS. I will be free of you.

II. 'Song of Soil'

WS. Today we plant nothing.
Before the sun climbs the eastern shore,
before our bodies dry out,
we will sprinkle thawed-out seeds
and press our ears to the ground.
Seven feet below raindrops and humus
our beating hearts will be felt,
the slight heat of our prayers will be felt,
until the sun guides my shadow across the valley's span.
Then I will walk to the giant rock that faces the sea
to take notes on last night's celestial observations:
grain-in-ear, summer solstice, slight rain, white dew,
the height of grass, a bosom of fruit.

WS—

grab a handful of the earth below your feet
and read it carefully
but do not try to analyse its structure.

You will not explain the song of soil
by indexing your analyses of its mineral composition.

Oh, WS:

I hear it whenever the sun rises,
a simple song coming from the clouds.

And always the chorus of trees and hills first.

Tide beating eternally.
Spring flowers.
Autumn fruits.
Our song.

Work at sunrise, rest at sunset
The sun is ahead of me, I am behind

WS, as my shovel hits the earth,
hear this song again—

Work at sunrise, rest at sunset
The sun is ahead of me, I am behind

———